6/0/1

ICE HOCKEY LEGENDS

Martin Brodeur

Sergei Fedorov

Peter Forsberg

Wayne Gretzky

Dominik Hasek

Brett Hull

Jaromir Jagr

Paul Kariya

John LeClair

Mario Lemieux

Eric Lindros

Mark Messier

CHELSEA HOUSE PUBLISHERS

ICE HOCKEY LEGENDS

PETER FORSBERG

Meg Greene

CHELSEA HOUSE PUBLISHERS
Philadelphia

Produced by P. M. Gordon Associates
Philadelphia, Pennsylvania

Picture research by Gillian Speeth, Picture This

CHELSEA HOUSE PUBLISHERS

Editor in Chief: Stephen Reginald
Managing Editor: James Gallagher
Production Manager: Pamela Loos
Art Director: Sara Davis
Director of Photography: Judy L. Hasday
Senior Production Editor: Lisa Chippendale
Publishing Coordinator: James McAvoy
Project Editor: Becky Durost Fish
Cover Design and Digital Illustration: Keith Trego

Cover Photos: front cover, portrait: Courtesy Colorado
Avalanche; front cover, action: AP/Wide World Photos; back
cover: Archive Photos

The Chelsea House World Wide Web site address is
http://www.chelseahouse.com

First Printing

1 3 5 7 9 8 6 4 2

Library of Congress Cataloging-in-Publication Data

Greene, Meg.
     Peter Forsberg / Meg Greene.
       p. cm. — (Ice hockey legends)
     Includes bibliographical references (p.) and index.
     Summary: A biography of the Swedish skater who scored
the gold medal-winning goal in the 1994 Olympics and went
on to play in the NHL for the Quebec Nordiques, later the
Colorado Avalanche.
     ISBN 0-7910-5013-0
     1. Forsberg, Peter, 1973– —Juvenile literature.
2. Hockey players—Sweden—Biography—Juvenile literature.
3. Colorado Avalanche (Hockey team)—Juvenile literature.
[1. Forsberg, Peter, 1973– . 2. Hockey players.] I. Title.
II. Series.
GV848.5.F67P48 1998
796.962'092—dc21   98-31353
[b]   CIP
                                                       AC

CONTENTS

THE STAMP GOAL

The score was 2–2. The deadlock seemed unbreakable, the game unending. How much longer could the players go on? How much more could the fans endure? After 60 minutes of regulation play and one 10-minute sudden-death overtime period, the outcome had yet to be decided.

The Swedish hockey team could hardly believe what was happening. Eyeing an Olympic gold medal in hockey for the first time in history, the underdog Swedes had battled their way past opponent after opponent at the 1994 winter Olympic Games held in Lillehammer, Norway. Now, in the final game against Team Canada, they were locked in a 2–2 tie. When Olympic officials told them the outcome would be settled by a "shoot-out," they felt the dream of winning a gold medal for Sweden slipping through their fingers.

Before the 1994 Olympics, Peter Forsberg was known as one of the two best players in the world who had not yet appeared in the National Hockey League. The Quebec Nordiques changed that.

The rules were simple. Each coach selected five players, each of whom would take one penalty shot at the opposing team's goalie. When all five players on each team had shot, the team with more goals would win the gold medal. If the score remained tied at the end of that first shoot-out round, the teams would proceed to a second. Neither team liked the odds. Mats Naslund, a Swedish player, later commented: "I hate the shoot-out. Too much luck involved." "That's no way to end a game," echoed Fabian Joseph, the captain of Team Canada.

Canada won the initial coin-toss and elected to shoot first. Petr Nedved, a Czech-born player who had become a Canadian citizen, began the shoot-out by whipping a shot past the Swedish goalie, Tommy Salo. Paul Kariya imitated Nedved's move and also scored for the Canadians. The Swedes failed on their first two attempts and trailed 2–0. Salo stopped the third Canadian shooter, Dwayne Norris, however, and likewise the fourth and fifth. In the meantime, Magnus Svensson and Peter Forsberg had scored for Team Sweden. At the end of the first five-shot round, the teams remained even.

With tension and exhaustion mounting, each team prepared to move to the next round. The pressure of the shoot-out was so great that two of Team Sweden's more seasoned players, Naslund and Hakan Loob, asked out of the second round after failing to score in the first. "They were scared," Swedish coach Curt Lundmark said later.

Svensson and Nedved each missed on their next attempts. As it turned out, the outcome rested on the shoulders of the two best players in the world who had not yet played in the National Hockey

League: the 19-year-old Kariya of Team Canada and the 20-year-old Forsberg of Team Sweden.

While the world watched, Forsberg readied himself to take his shot. Despite a lackluster performance at the beginning of the Olympics, Forsberg had blasted his way through the semifinal game against heavily favored Russia, contributing three impressive assists that helped secure a 4–3 win.

Forsberg may have been skating in Lillehammer, but in his mind he was replaying the 1989 World Hockey Championships, where the great Swedish player Kent Nilsson, one of Forsberg's idols, had scored the winning goal with a spectacular shot on a breakaway. "I liked [Nilsson's winning shot] right away," Forsberg later recalled—"the goalie ended up in the stands." Forsberg decided to imitate Nilsson's shot in the shoot-out against Team Canada. With so much riding on a single

The famous "Stamp Goal," February 27, 1994: After a spectacular change of direction, Forsberg flips the puck one-handed past Canadian goaltender Corey Hirsch, winning the Olympic gold medal for Sweden.

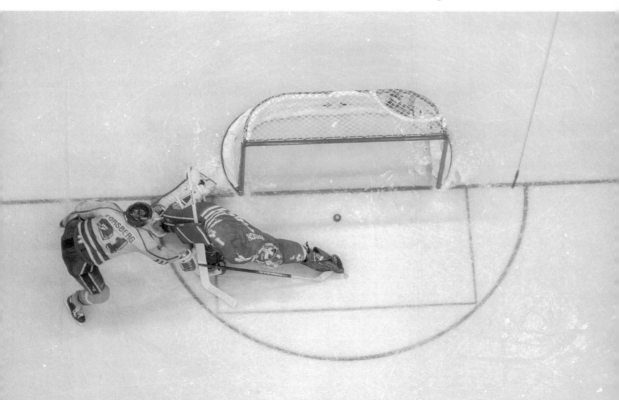

Sweden's hockey players celebrate their gold medal at the 1994 winter Olympic Games. In back stand the defeated Canadians.

attempt, it was perhaps not the time to try something fancy. But Forsberg weighed the risks and resolved to do it.

Skating slowly toward Corey Hirsch, Team Canada's netminder, Forsberg, a left-handed shooter, swooped to the left on his forehand. He picked up speed. Hirsch followed his movements, trying to anticipate what he would do next. Suddenly Forsberg shifted directions. Skating almost to the goal crease, he drew the puck to his backhand (right) side and behind him. Hirsch dropped to his knees and stretched out his glove hand to make the save. But with only his right hand on the stick, Forsberg reached back and tapped the puck into the net, past the sprawling Hirsch. It was a magnificent goal. Swedish hockey fans erupted in jubilation.

The Swedish players, however, weren't quite ready to celebrate yet. Anxiously they watched as Paul Kariya skated toward Tommy Salo. He faked Salo out of position, then fired the puck high, hoping to elevate it above Salo's glove hand. But Salo recovered with lightning quickness; the puck bounced harmlessly away.

What had arguably been the most exciting game in the history of Olympic hockey was over. Team Sweden had its gold medal.

When asked later about his winning shot, Forsberg modestly admitted that he had tried the move "three times before." How many times had it succeeded? "None," he replied. But earlier failures didn't matter now. "Whatever happened out there, I was going to put the puck in the net," Forsberg said. "I had no doubt in my mind that I was going to score."

Peter's coach, Curt Lundmark, had not been so confident. "Any other player would get two years in jail if he attempted such a penalty shot," he joked.

Forsberg's historic goal became so celebrated in Sweden that the moment has been immortalized on a postage stamp. The goal itself has become known as the "Stamp Goal." Forsberg, though, shares the credit for his success with his team. "I don't see that stamp as just for me. I see it as a symbol for the whole team winning the goal."

Peter Forsberg's memorable Olympic perfor-

Peter Forsberg displays his Olympic gold medal at Lillehammer, Norway.

mance signaled an important turning point in his young hockey career. The Quebec Nordiques of the National Hockey League (NHL) had already signed him to a four-year, $6.5-million contract. The Nordiques, having finished with a disappointing 34–42–8 record during the 1993–94 NHL season, had failed to make the playoffs. The organization was pinning high hopes on Forsberg to transform the club into a perennial contender for the Stanley Cup, the NHL's championship trophy.

Was Forsberg up to the task? Marcel Aubut, owner of the Quebec Nordiques, thought so. Aubut was impressed with his future center. "He showed he's a player when it counts," Aubut commented. "This is a 20-year-old player with the weight of his country on his shoulders and a gold medal in his hand." Mats Naslund, one of Forsberg's Swedish teammates, said of Forsberg's Olympic performance, "For the first time, he proved to me that he's not only a promising player but he's ready to play in the big games." Now Forsberg had to live up to those words.

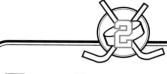

THE PURSUIT OF EXCELLENCE

Winter in Ornskoldsvik, Sweden, is long, cold, and dark. Located approximately 300 miles north of Stockholm, Ornskoldsvik, which means "Eagle Shield by the Bay," is so near the Arctic Circle that during the winter the sun shines only a few hours every day.

To pass the dreary winter months more agreeably, the 60,000 or so citizens of Ornskoldsvik have made a habit of telling stories. One of the most popular tales, repeated so often that over the years it has become a local legend, involves a farmer named Henneng Sandvquist from nearby Norra, Sweden, who was capable of performing feats of amazing strength. Such ability apparently runs in Sandvquist's family, for his grandson, Peter Forsberg, would soon begin to perform some astonishing feats of his own. Another Ornskoldsvik legend was in the making.

Besides storytelling, hockey is the other pre-

As a youth, Peter Forsberg showed the intensity that has marked his play ever since.

15

ferred wintertime activity in Ornskoldsvik. In fact, hockey is so popular there that children begin learning how to skate almost as soon as they can walk. Hockey is a particularly strong tradition in the Forsberg household. Peter's father, Kent Forsberg, formerly a well-known professional hockey player in Sweden, is now the head coach of the Swedish national team. Peter's older brother, Roger, also played hockey. So it was no surprise that the young Forsberg had taken to the ice by the time he was four years old.

Looking back, Peter credits his father as the strongest influence on his career. "He was good both on and off the ice. He was my coach for a long time, and we never had any fights. We kept hockey down at the rink. When we got home we didn't even talk about it." Forsberg also credits his father for not pushing him to play if he didn't want to but, at the same time, always insisting that Peter do his best whenever he stepped onto the ice.

Peter needed little encouragement. He wanted to play. He followed his father and his older brother to their practices. When Peter was a boy, Kent coached a junior team in Ornskoldsvik on which both his sons played. Roger Forsberg, two years older than Peter, made the competition keen. At first, keeping up with Roger was hard for young Peter. Their father made sure that he showed no favoritism toward either boy. If Peter wanted to play hockey, he would have to excel even against boys who were older, stronger, and more agile than he was, including his brother.

Despite the rivalry that grew up between them, Peter and Roger had a good relationship. Peter remembered that "it was like anything else, always fighting for things—it was pretty funny. He was a

good player, so it was pretty natural for me to fol-
low along. He was better than me in everything in
the beginning, but we were pretty even after a
while." That equality did not last long. Soon
enough, Peter, though still very young, began to
display the exceptional hockey skills that forever
set him apart from most of his peers.

Growing up, Peter admired his father and brother, but he also had other idols. His favorite was
fellow countryman Hakan Loob, the exciting right
winger who scored 50 goals for the Calgary Flames
during the 1987–88 season. At that time, Loob

*Peter with his father, Kent
Forsberg, a coach and former professional player.*

was the only Swede playing in the National Hockey League. One of Peter's greatest thrills came in 1994, when he skated alongside the veteran Loob on the Swedish Olympic team.

Another player whom Forsberg admired was Kent Nilsson. Like Loob, Nilsson had also played in the NHL. In 1989, when Peter was 15 and still playing for his junior league team, he watched as Nilsson scored a dramatic backhanded goal against Team USA to win the World Championships. It was that incredible move that Forsberg successfully imitated five years later with his famous penalty shot at the 1994 Olympics.

Because NHL games were infrequently televised in Sweden, Forsberg had only a passing knowledge of some of the North American stars of the league. He admitted to never having seen Wayne Gretzky play "a whole game" until he arrived in the United States.

Although Peter's heroes were hockey players, he himself did not yet know how far his talents could carry him, or how far he wanted them to. For young hockey players in Sweden, life was often demanding. Combining school with hockey was serious business. In an interview, Forsberg described the typical instruction that young Swedes undergo: "You have your regular classes, like three hours every other day, three times a week. You get twice a week to have an ice practice. Once a week you have weight lifting."

Keeping up with such a busy schedule wasn't easy; it required dedication and sacrifice. Yet Peter now remembers this time in his life as enjoyable. "It was great," he said. "Every practice was hard . . . like a war." He believes that this tough training helped him a great deal.

It did not take Forsberg long to make up his mind about the future. He would do whatever was necessary to become the best hockey player he could be. Early on, therefore, he began to display the grit and determination on and off the ice that have made him unwilling to settle for second best.

Forsberg made his first television appearance in 1988 during the *TV-pucken,* a Swedish hockey tournament among the different *landskap,* or districts. The average age of the competitors in the *TV-pucken* is 15 years. Many future Swedish hockey stars have received their first national exposure during this yearly tournament. Peter was no exception.

By the time he had turned 16 years old, it was apparent that Peter had overtaken his brother as well as several other junior players in Ornskoldsvik. He decided to test his abilities in the Swedish *Elitserien,* the Elite League, widely considered the best professional league in the world next to the NHL. He wanted to try out for the MoDo team, one of the most celebrated franchises in the history of Swedish hockey.

The coach of the MoDo squad, however, felt that Peter wasn't yet big enough or strong enough to play in the Elite League. He suggested that Peter work out with weights to improve his strength and conditioning. Though disappointed at being refused a place on the team, Peter took the coach's advice and joined a gym. He began a rigorous daily regime of exercise and weight-lifting. At the same time, he perfected his hockey skills, never gave up on himself, and never lost sight of his goal.

Peter's hard work paid off. On November 4, 1990, the now 17-year-old Forsberg made his professional debut with MoDo of the Swedish Elite

*By the age of 17, Peter Fors-
berg (left) made his professional debut with the MoDo
team in the Swedish Elite
League.*

League. He soon was playing regularly, displaying the skill and finesse that would quickly mark
him as a world-class player. By the end of his first
season, Forsberg had amassed 17 points, scoring
7 goals and assisting on 10 others. Even though
he had played in only 25 games of the 40-game
schedule, Forsberg ranked eighth overall in scoring for the MoDo club.

In addition to scoring, Forsberg was already
developing the hard-hitting style of play more characteristic of North American than European hockey. "Peter always played with older guys, and he

wanted to show them he could give a hit and take a hit," his father recalled. "Sometimes he was a little too physical."

Another characteristic of Peter's game was his strong skating. It was becoming virtually impossible for an opposing player to knock him off the puck. In addition, his confident puck-handling and utter fearlessness were beginning to earn him second looks from visiting NHL scouts.

Even Wayne Gretzky, of whom Forsberg knew little, had heard of him. Before the 1994 Olympic Games, Gretzky identified Forsberg as the "best young player in the world" not yet playing in the National Hockey League. All of this attention was bound to arouse curiosity across the Atlantic. The NHL was beckoning.

THE MAGIC BOY

"**W**ith the first pick in the 1991 Entry Draft," announced Gary Bettman, commissioner of the National Hockey League, "the Quebec Nordiques select Eric Lindros." Although no one suspected it at the time, those words changed not only Lindros's life but also Peter Forsberg's.

Hurting for good players and having dreams of winning their first Stanley Cup, the Nordiques had chosen the big and talented Lindros. The only problem was that Lindros refused to play for Marcel Aubut, owner of the Nordiques. He believed the Nordiques weren't serious about building a winning team. "I told him he didn't know me if he said that, and he didn't know the other people in the organization," responded General Manager Pierre Page.

Lindros, born and raised in London, Ontario, also had misgivings about playing and living in a French-speaking city. Rather than sign with the

---

Even after being selected in the 1991 NHL draft, Forsberg continued to play in Europe.

Nordiques, he sat out his first year of NHL eligibility in the hope of being traded to another team. During that time, he played for the Canadian team that won the silver medal in the 1992 Olympics at Albertville, France.

As draft day of 1992 approached, general managers and coaches around the NHL heard rumors that the Nordiques would listen to offers for Eric Lindros. When these rumors were confirmed, the activity became frenzied. Offers for Lindros came from almost every team in the league. In fact, the bidding for Lindros grew so frenetic that the Nordiques found themselves making deals for Lindros with *both* the New York Rangers and the Philadelphia Flyers!

The Flyers won the rights to Lindros in the end, but at a high price. In order to obtain Lindros, the Flyers had to give up a number of young players and high draft picks. Goalie Ron Hextall, center Mike Ricci, defensemen Steve Duchesne and Kerry Huffman, left wing Chris Simon, first-round draft picks in 1993 and 1994, and $15 million sealed the deal. The Nordiques also insisted on obtaining the rights to Peter Forsberg, who, almost one month shy of his eighteenth birthday, had been picked in the first round by the Flyers with the sixth overall selection of 1991.

"It felt funny to be traded even before I had played a game in the NHL," Forsberg later recalled, "but when I heard Eric Lindros, I knew it was a big deal. I had heard much about Lindros in Sweden, almost as much as Wayne Gretzky."

Winnipeg agent Don Baizley spent three months working out the arrangements between the Nordiques and the Flyers. He demanded the right for Forsberg not only to play in the Olympic Games with Team Sweden, but also to finish his season with MoDo in the Swedish Elite League.

The Nordiques, agreeing to these conditions, offered Forsberg a $6.5-million contract for four seasons—over $1.6 million a year. This sum was vastly greater than the $80,000 he was making with MoDo, and it made him the highest-paid Swedish hockey player ever.

The terms of Peter's contract did not escape the notice of his new teammates. When asked about possible resentment, Forsberg replied, "Of course I care about how they react to me, but if they were me, they would do the same. I'm told they [the Nordiques' players] should be glad I signed a big contract, because the next time they could sign one too."

Although Forsberg had been largely overlooked in the drama and controversy surrounding the Lindros trade, early reports mentioned an up-and-coming young player in Sweden who was the key to the transaction for the Nordiques. "Even before the Junior Worlds, we were being told by Swedish hockey observers, who can be very conservative in their assessments of young players, that this was the best player ever to come out of Sweden," recalled Pierre Page, then the Nordiques' general manager and coach. He went on, "I won't say Peter will be a Lindros, but I don't think this franchise is ever going to kick itself for making the trade."

Anders Hedberg, a scout for the Toronto Maple Leafs and a former Swedish hockey player, thought Forsberg "had the same incredible determination that I hadn't seen . . . since Ulf Nilsson," one of Sweden's great hockey legends. Nilsson himself, who once saw Forsberg score 10 points in a game against Team Japan in the 1993 World Junior championship, was equally impressed. "I have not seen a player of Forsberg's caliber in a long time," he said. "If Quebec keeps him, they're going to be the team of the '90s."

Nevertheless, Forsberg didn't pack his bags for Quebec immediately. He refused to be seduced by the prospect of money or fame. He believed he was not ready to play in the NHL, and he would not become a member of the Nordiques until he was. "I didn't feel mature enough . . . , and I just wanted to stay home. And I had school to finish there," Forsberg said.

Peter worried, in fact, that he might not be good enough to play in the NHL. With that possibility in mind, he wanted to prepare for a career in economics, just in case.

He continued to play hockey in Sweden, though, dominating the Elite League like no player before. The young man who was once advised that he was not big or strong enough to play for MoDo was now rapidly gaining a reputation as a player to be reckoned with. He was not known for scoring "pretty" goals, but he was noticed for his playmaking ability and his relentless pursuit of the puck—as well as his pursuit of opponents. He would backcheck, hook, hold, hack—do anything and everything to keep the other team from scoring. Forsberg put it simply: "I hate losing. I can't stand losing."

During the 1992–93 season, Forsberg also helped lead Sweden to the World Junior championship. Personally, the tournament was a tremendous success for Peter. He scored 7 goals and had 24 assists in just 7 games. With a total of 31 points, he set a new tournament record. He also received the Best Player award at the conclusion of the tournament. Indeed, Forsberg was touted as the

*Ignoring the blandish-
ments of the NHL, Fors-
berg (far left) plays for
Team Sweden in the 1993
Izvestia Cup tournament.*

most dominant player in the history of the World
Junior Tournament.

After the tournament, Forsberg continued to
stand out in regular-season play for MoDo. By
now, however, his rugged style of play—running
opponents into the boards and leveling them with
crushing open-ice hits—was making him something of an outcast among Swedish players. Vet-
erans compared the experience to "getting sucker-
punched by some punk." Even Peter's father, Kent,
admitted that Peter was considered too rough-
and-tumble by many of the players in the Swedish
Elite League. In 1991, during Peter's second season with MoDo, an article in the Swedish national daily *Aftonbladet* lamented his rough play, along

with that of linemate Markus Naslund. The news-paper headline read: "THEY MUST BE STOPPED!"

In an effort to teach Forsberg a lesson, many of the older players provoked him, hoping to throw him off his game or lure him into earning penalties. But Peter never backed down, and by his last season in Sweden, 1993–94, many of his rivals had actually started to respect him.

Peter's tireless pursuit of excellence was amply rewarded. In 1992 and 1993, he won the *Guldhjalmen*, an annual award given to the best hockey player in Sweden, as determined by the players' own voting. In both of those years, he also won the coveted *Guldpucken*, an annual award given by the Swedish newspaper *Expressen*. Until then, no player had ever received the *Guldpucken* more than once.

At this point Forsberg had nothing more to prove in Sweden, and he decided it was now time to move on to Quebec, the Nordiques, and the National Hockey League. Unfortunately, circumstances beyond his control delayed his debut in the NHL.

In the fall of 1994, just before the start of the NHL season, team owners canceled all games and "locked out" the players, thus preventing them from playing even if they wanted to do so. At stake were a number of economic issues that the players and owners had been haggling over for the last year and a half. The owners wanted to limit player salaries and to control free agency, the players' right to move from one team to another. The players, in contrast, demanded greater freedom to sign with other teams at the end of their contracts. The players also wanted a larger percentage of the profits from the sale of hockey merchandise such as team sweaters, shirts, posters, hats, and other memorabilia.

The lockout lasted for nearly four months, until January 1995, when the owners and players at last agreed to a compromise. That year, there would be a shortened training camp, then an abbreviated season consisting of 48 games, followed by a full playoff schedule. Peter was finally going to get his chance to play with the best players in the world.

At first, he faced the inevitable concerns about his ability to adapt to the physical style of play that characterizes North American hockey. Despite their tremendous skills, European players were still stereotyped as too "soft" physically for the hard-hitting style of hockey common among many American and Canadian players.

Ironically, Forsberg's NHL debut pitted him against Eric Lindros, the very player whose fate had been entwined with his. Forsberg immediately lined up the 6'4", 234-pound center and tried to drive him into the boards. Forsberg, who stands only 6' and weighs only 190 pounds, got the worst of the exchange. Yet his teammates were impressed with his courage and determination. Wendel Clark told him: "Peter, you'll do fine. That's the hardest check you'll ever get in this league." Quebec went on to win the game, 3–1.

Soon Forsberg had demonstrated conclusively that the view of European players as "soft" was mistaken. "You can't knock him off the puck," noted teammate Joe Sakic. As one broadcaster put it, "When Peter has the puck, you have to cheat to get it from him." Coach Marc Crawford later observed that "a lot of Europeans have that knock on them that they're soft, but Peter would give as much as he'd take. He's just one of those players that don't come around very often."

Besides displaying the toughness, speed,

strength, and style that are the hallmarks of great NHL players, Forsberg possessed an eerie sense of where other players were on the ice. Like Wayne Gretzky, he could thread a pass to his teammates with pinpoint precision. This gifted stickhandling, combined with his speed and strength, brought him to the attention of teammates, opponents, coaches, and fans alike.

In a February 1995 game, John Gruden of the Boston Bruins (left) helps Forsberg learn about the NHL's physical style of play.

During that first NHL season, Forsberg established himself as one of the best young players in the league, accumulating 50 points, on 15 goals and 35 assists, in only 47 games. One of the few criticisms that could be made was that he proved to be a reluctant shooter. His 15 goals came on only 86 shots. "I'm just not a natural goal-scorer," he explained later. "That's probably why I pass more than I shoot it. If you're a good goal-scorer," he went on, "I think you've got a different attitude. . . . I think you have to be a bit selfish [to score goals]. But I'm not."

In his personal life, Forsberg was not bothered by the culture shock that has frequently troubled European players during their first years in the NHL. He liked Quebec, even though the city and the people seemed strange to him and he could not speak or understand one word of French. Since Quebec had only one major sport, the media attention and pressure on Forsberg were intense. But he appreciated the fans' support and enthusiasm, remaining modest no matter how lavishly they or the sportswriters praised him. "I don't really like talking about myself," he said in one interview. He preferred instead to talk about the game, his teammates, or his opponents. Reporters were not put off. They dubbed him "The Magic Boy," after the title of a Swedish biography, and scrutinized every aspect of his life.

Perhaps surprisingly, Forsberg still had doubts about making it in the NHL. "At the beginning of the season I didn't play very well at all. For a while I felt at any minute I might be sent to the farm team." Despite these misgivings, Forsberg's rookie season proved that he did indeed have the talent to play in the NHL. His 50 points ranked him

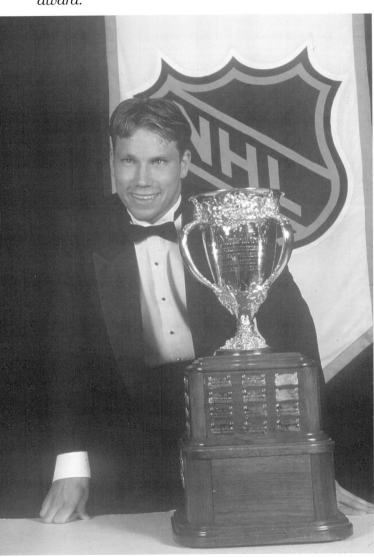

Forsberg accepts the Calder Trophy as the NHL's Rookie of the Year. He was the first Swedish player to win the award.

17th in the league in scoring. His plus/minus rating of +17 indicated strong defensive skills to complement his potent offense. (A player receives a "plus" point if he is on the ice when his club scores an even-strength or shorthanded goal. A player receives a "minus" point if he is on the ice when the opposing club scores an even-strength or shorthanded goal. A high plus/minus rating, such as Forsberg's, usually indicates effective play on both offense and defense.)

As a fitting cap for the season, Peter Forsberg became the first Swedish player to win the coveted Calder Trophy awarded to the Rookie of the Year. "That's a big thing back home," said Forsberg of the award. "To be the first Swedish winner means a lot to me and the Swedish people."

Did Forsberg ever dwell on the circumstances, particularly his trade from the Flyers for Eric Lindros, that brought him to Quebec? "As much as people want to make [it] him against me, that wasn't the trade, just a part of it," Forsberg said in an interview. "I cannot worry about Eric Lindros every night. I have to be myself and do things that will help the team." In fact, being himself and playing his own brand of hockey had enabled Forsberg to complete his first NHL season with better numbers than the much-acclaimed Lindros.

At 23, he had already begun to make his mark. What more could he want? The answer to that question was easy: to hoist the Stanley Cup.

BUILDING A
CHAMPION

The New York Rangers were in a surly mood. Having won their first Stanley Cup in 54 years the previous season, the Rangers had struggled during the lockout-shortened 1994–95 campaign, finishing with a record of 22 wins, 23 losses, and 3 ties, which barely qualified them for the playoffs. In the meantime, with Forsberg and the other players acquired in the trade with Philadelphia, the Nordiques had compiled the best record in the Eastern Conference, 30–13–5. These two teams were matched in the first round of the playoffs.

Their own success, combined with the Rangers' regular-season woes, gave the young Nordiques a sense of confidence. But the Broadway Blueshirts soon changed that feeling to disappointment. Led by fiery captain Mark Messier, smooth-skating defenseman Brian Leetch, and reliable goaltender Mike Richter, the veteran Rangers defeated the Nordiques, eliminating them from the playoffs.

Forsberg (left) checks the New Jersey Devils' Neal Broten during an early game of the 1995–96 season.

Even with the addition of Forsberg to the line-up, Pierre Lacroix, the new general manager of the Nordiques, realized that the team was not yet ready to compete with the elite clubs of the National Hockey League. He had work to do during the off-season if he wanted to avoid another frustratingly early exit from the playoffs.

Compounding the Nordiques' on-ice problems, though, were the persistent financial difficulties of the organization. The franchise had suffered money troubles for some time. The Nordiques wanted a new arena that would help boost attendance and bring in the greater revenues needed to sign talented free agents, make key trades, and keep the skilled players already on the roster. But in a referendum on the proposed new arena, city residents had voted the idea down, and the team had begun looking for another home.

Even before the playoffs ended in that spring of 1995, news reports surfaced that the Quebec Nordiques were to be sold to the Ascent Entertainment Group and that the new owners intended to move the team to Denver, Colorado. Although Nordiques fans were displeased, there was little they could do to prevent the inevitable, and the sale took place. The franchise prepared to relocate to its new home in the Rockies, where it would become known as the Colorado Avalanche.

The new ownership group assured Lacroix that the money was now available to improve the team. Lacroix pinpointed three key improvements that the team needed to become a Stanley Cup contender: first, better leadership; second, more offense, especially from the defensemen; and third, a more experienced goaltender.

Less than a month after the team moved to Denver, and just days before the start of the

1995–96 season, Lacroix found one of the missing pieces of his puzzle. He acquired veteran right winger Claude Lemieux, the winner of the 1995 Conn Smythe Trophy as the Most Valuable Player in the playoffs. Involved in a contract dispute with the Stanley Cup champion New Jersey Devils, Lemieux had demanded a trade. Lacroix was happy to help the Devils solve their problem. In a three-way deal, the Devils sent Lemieux to the New York Islanders in exchange for veteran left winger Steve Thomas. The Islanders then traded Lemieux to the Avalanche for rugged left winger Wendel Clark. At the time he became a member of the Avalanche, Lemieux had already seen his name twice inscribed on the Stanley Cup.

Before the season was a month old, Lacroix engineered his second major deal, acquiring offensive defenseman Sandis Ozolinsh from the San Jose Sharks in exchange for the tough and talented forward Owen Nolan. This transaction helped the Avalanche overcome the devastating loss of defenseman Uwe Krupp, who had suffered a knee injury in the very first game of the season. The addition of Ozolinsh not only helped to offset Krupp's absence, but immediately made the Avalanche power play one of the best in the league.

The most important trade of all, however, was the one Lacroix pulled off on December 6, 1995. He snatched the talented but disgruntled goaltender Patrick Roy, along with hard-hitting defensive forward Mike Keane, from the Montreal Cana-

As the Nordiques moved to Colorado to become the Avalanche, General Manager Pierre Lacroix was charged with improving the team.

One of the Avalanche's key acquisitions in 1995 was star goaltender Patrick Roy, shown here playing for Team Canada in the 1998 Olympics.

diens for backup goaltender Jocelyn Thibault, left winger Martin Rucinsky, and forward Andrei Kovalenko. Keane, the respected captain of the Canadiens' squad, had run afoul of the French-speaking fans and media in Montreal when he said he did not think it necessary for him to learn French. Roy, already twice the Most Valuable Player of the playoffs, felt coach Mario Tremblay had deliberately embarrassed him during a game against the Detroit Red Wings by not relieving him until he had given up seven goals in an eventual 11–0 shellacking. Furious, Roy declared he had played his last game for the Canadiens, and within days he and Keane were dealt to Colorado.

When Jimmy Devellano, senior vice-president of hockey operations for the rival Red Wings, learned of the trade that brought Roy and Keane to the Avalanche, he reportedly wept.

Lacroix, for his part, believed that he at last had the players to go all the way to the Stanley Cup finals. He had the coach as well: Marc Crawford, now in his second year at the helm, had won the Jack Adams Trophy as the Coach of the Year. All things considered, the Avalanche seemed ready set to make a serious run at the Cup.

WINNING
THE CUP

For Peter Forsberg, the move to Denver meant not only a new city, but also a new country, new ownership, new teammates, new uniform, and another new beginning.

In the first few days of practice at the Avalanche training camp, Forsberg found that the thin mountain air burned his lungs and often left him gasping for breath. This was one other change to which he would have to become accustomed.

Other than getting acclimated to the altitude and having to drink more water, however, Forsberg was having a good time in Denver. "There's a lot to do and see," he told reporters. He showed great excitement and curiosity about his new home, asking such questions as "Where's the best place to go in the mountains?" and "What are the winters like?" He was also eager to discover the best places to fish.

Two big questions, however, awaited an answer

For Peter Forsberg, the 1995–96 season was truly one to celebrate. Here he reacts to his first goal in Game 2 of the Stanley Cup finals.

as Forsberg entered his second season in the NHL. First, after playing in only 47 games during the lockout-shortened 1994–95 season, was he up to a grueling regular schedule of more than 80 games? Second, would he be prone to the "sophomore slump" experienced by so many other young players after a spectacular rookie season?

Forsberg did not expect the longer slate of games or the sophomore jinx to affect the quality of his play. "I'm a pretty simple guy," he said in one interview. "I just like to do my job and that's it." Yet he realized that his second year would be different from his first in many ways: "It's going to be a lot harder this year. Guys have been telling me what to expect and I know it will be harder." Opposing teams are "going to come at me a little harder, and I know that."

Concerning Forsberg, Avalanche coach Marc Crawford predicted that "the people of Denver are in for a real treat." And Forsberg didn't disappoint them. Along with teammate Joe Sakic, Forsberg made the franchise's debut in Colorado exciting for fans and players alike. In the first month of the season, the Avalanche skated to a league-best 9–0–1 record, letting everyone know that there was a new team to contend with in the Western Conference.

By the end of the regular season, the Avalanche had cruised to a first-place finish in the Pacific Division with a record of 47 wins, 25 losses, and 10 ties, amassing a total of 104 points—25 points more than the second-place Calgary Flames. The Avalanche's tremendous season was overshadowed only by that of the Red Wings, who won an NHL-record 62 games and accumulated 131 points.

Forsberg's individual performance mirrored that

March 1996: With Forsberg helping to lead the way, the Avalanche drive to a first-place finish in the Pacific Division.

of his team. He had struck for 116 points on 30 goals and 86 assists, placing him fifth in overall league scoring. Along with teammate Joe Sakic, Forsberg became one of two Avalanche players to appear in all 82 regular-season games. He would also compete in all 22 playoff games.

At the end of the regular season, Sakic called Forsberg "the most complete player in the game. Both ends of the ice. He's so strong defensively and so unselfish." General Manager Lacroix characterized Forsberg as "a magician. When he has the puck on his stick, it's impossible to get [it] away [from him]. And when he goes after the puck, he gets it—always." Events in the playoffs would make Sakic and Lacroix look like prophets.

Entering the playoffs, the team had not forgotten the discouraging loss to the Rangers a year earlier. To a man, each player felt he had something to prove to rest of the league and to his teammates. "It was the most frustrating summer I ever had," Sakic declared. "All summer I couldn't wait to get back on the ice."

Forsberg scores against Canucks goalie Corey Hirsch during the opening round of the 1996 playoffs.

The first test came in the playoffs' opening round against the Vancouver Canucks. The Avalanche kicked off the series with a 5–2 win, but the Canucks made the most of Gino Odjick's first two career playoff goals to take Game 2 by a score of 5–4. The teams split the next two games in Vancouver, with the Avalanche winning the third game 4–0 behind Roy's superb goaltending, and the Canucks rebounding once more to take Game 4 by a score of 4–3.

The teams returned to Colorado with the series tied at two games apiece. In Game 5 Sakic scored a hat trick (three goals in one game), including the game winner 51 seconds into overtime, giving the Avalanche a 3–2 lead in the series. From that point, Colorado never looked back. The 'Lanche finished the series quickly, taking Game 6 by a score of 3–2. The triumph marked the first playoff series victory for the Nordiques/Avalanche franchise since 1987.

In the next round the Avalanche went on to roust the Chicago Blackhawks in another hard-fought six-game series. Four of those games were decided in overtime. For the first time in 11 years, the franchise had advanced to the third round of the playoffs.

So far in the playoffs, Forsberg's play had been stellar. Although Sakic, Roy, and Lemieux grabbed the headlines, Forsberg had quietly gone about his business. By the conclusion of the series against the Blackhawks, sportswriters, commentators, players, and fans had begun to remark not only on Forsberg's goal-scoring and puck-handling, but also on his checking, hitting, and generally strong defensive play. It was becoming clear that Peter Forsberg was more than just an offensive threat.

He could not have chosen a better moment to elevate his game. In the tough conference final against the Detroit Red Wings, the Avalanche would need every weapon in their arsenal.

In Game 1 against the Red Wings, Mike Keane netted the winning goal at 17:31 in overtime. In Game 2 Roy made 35 saves, enabling the Avalanche to shut out the Wings, 3–0, taking a two-game advantage in the series.

The Wings responded by winning Game 3, 6–4, behind three assists from Sergei Fedorov. The Avalanche then put a seeming stranglehold on the series with a 4–2 victory in Game 4. The Red Wings' backs were against the wall—one more loss would finish them. They responded by winning Game 5 by a score of 5–2. It was their 72nd victory of the season.

During this series, Forsberg had again been lauded for his rugged physical play, particularly on defense. He had almost completely shut down Detroit's high-scoring centers, Sergei Fedorov, Steve Yzerman, and Igor Larionov. In the decisive Game 6, though, it was Forsberg himself who took over the Avalanche attack. He scored the game-winning goal by "nutmegging" Wings star defenseman Nicklas Lidstrom, gliding the puck between Lidstrom's legs and then firing it under the pads of the helpless goalie, Chris Osgood. The Avalanche won that game 4–1 to advance to the Stanley Cup finals against the surprising Eastern Conference champions, the Florida Panthers.

After the long road to the finals, the last stage went quickly. Relying on the same combination of finesse and toughness that had defined their magical season, the Avalanche devastated the Panthers in four games to capture the Stanley Cup. For the only time in hockey history, a team had won the Stanley Cup in its first year in a new city. For all the players who had suffered as Nordiques through the monotonous years of losing, the victory was sweeter for being so long overdue.

Throughout that final series, Forsberg had continued his brilliant play. Facing off against tough and experienced Panthers center Brian Skrudland, Forsberg dished out at least as much punishment as he took. Of the rough and relentless body checking, Forsberg said: "I can handle that as long as we're winning. I can take any beating."

Forsberg's 10 playoff goals included a hat trick in Game 2 against the Panthers—all 3 goals coming in the first 10:56 of the opening period! The first came on a rebound shot that caromed off the stick of Panthers defenseman Rhett Warrener. Forsberg redirected the puck past goaltender John Vanbiesbrouck. For his second goal, Forsberg blasted a heavy wrist shot from the left faceoff circle, beating Vanbiesbrouck on the glove side. The hat-trick goal came when the puck caromed off the end boards and ended up on Forsberg's stick; he easily swatted it by the luckless Vanbiesbrouck.

Forsberg's hat trick decided the outcome before that game was 11 minutes old. The Avalanche won in a rout, 8–1. Following the game, teammate Mike Keane said simply, "Good to see him shoot." But hockey historians knew the feat was something special. Only five other players had scored hat tricks in the Stanley Cup finals: "Busher" Jackson of Toronto in 1932, "Terrible Ted" Lindsay of Detroit in 1955, Maurice "Rocket" Richard of Montreal in 1957, Wayne Gretzky of Edmonton in 1985, and Dirk Graham of Chicago in 1992. All except Gretzky, who is still playing, and Graham, who is ineligible for election because he has only recently retired, are in the Hockey Hall of Fame.

In Game 3 Sakic had the game-winner as the Avalanche prevailed 3–2. Forsberg contributed an assist and carried on his dominant physical play, beating the grinding Panthers at their own game.

The final game of the 1995–96 Stanley Cup finals, played in Miami Arena, was a classic. Through the 60 minutes of regulation time, the teams were knotted at 0–0. They played one extra session. Still no score. They went to a second overtime. The results were the same. At the end of five periods, 100 minutes of hockey, neither team had managed to score a goal.

Finally, at 4:31 of the sixth period, the third overtime, Avalanche defenseman Uwe Krupp, who had returned from reconstructive knee surgery in time for the playoffs, ended the longest game in the history of the National Hockey League with a slapshot that sailed by Vanbiesbrouck into the net. The Avalanche had won the Stanley Cup.

Joe Sakic was named Most Valuable Player and awarded the Conn Smythe Trophy, but coaches, players, writers, and fans agreed that without Forsberg's timely goal-scoring and gritty defensive play, there might never have been a Stanley Cup celebration in Colorado. Even Florida Panthers general manager Bryan Murray agreed, saying, "I don't think there was any question he [Forsberg] was the best player." Patrick Roy offered the diplomatic statement that Forsberg and Sakic were "the best forwards I've ever played with."

That summer, Peter Forsberg had a chance to celebrate the Avalanche victory and his own accomplishments when the Stanley Cup arrived at his home in Ornskoldsvik. According to the bylaws of the National Hockey League, every player on the winning club gets to keep the Stanley Cup for three days. Forsberg insisted that the Cup

Hat trick! Forsberg cele-brates his third goal of Game 2 in the Stanley Cup finals.

come to his hometown before traveling to Stockholm, the capital of Sweden. Swedish hockey fans didn't really care where in the country the Cup made its appearance. Peter Forsberg—whom they called Foppa, or "Puck Wizard"—had brought them another thrill and another first, for the Cup had never before been on Swedish soil.

In keeping with his modest and unassuming personality, Forsberg did not plan a big ceremony to mark the arrival of the Cup. Instead, he took it along on a picnic with family and friends.

PETER
THE GREAT

Immediately after his picnic with the Stanley Cup, Peter Forsberg went off to play for Team Sweden in the World Cup of Hockey. Soon thereafter it was time for a new NHL season.

During that next season, 1996–97, Forsberg continued to play a dazzling brand of hockey. After only two years in the league, he was being readily compared to some of the greatest legends of the game, including Gordie Howe of the Detroit Red Wings, whom many believe was the best two-way forward in the history of the sport.

"Any time Forsberg wants, he can step up the tempo and take control," said former Chicago Blackhawks goaltender and current ESPN hockey analyst Darren Pang. Goalie Martin Brodeur of the New Jersey Devils described Forsberg as "patient and creative." He will "lull you to sleep before he bites you like a snake," Brodeur con-

In the give-and-take of NHL hockey, Forsberg often takes as much as he gives—and for that reason, his career has been hampered by injuries.

tinued. "He has that tremendous flair for [creating] opportunities."

The quality of Forsberg's play was all the more impressive since he had to deal with nagging injuries for the first time in his career. A severe thigh injury sidelined him for 17 games during 1996–97. Yet he still finished the season with 28 goals and 58 assists for a total of 86 points in only 65 games. His plus/minus rating of +31—his highest yet in the NHL—attested to his consistently strong defensive play.

At the end of a magnificent season in which the team won the President's Trophy for having the best record in the NHL (49–24–9), the Avalanche prepared to defend the Stanley Cup. Although Forsberg and team captain Joe Sakic had missed a total of 34 games because of injury, the Avalanche were healthy going into the playoffs.

In the opening round, they dispatched a determined but undermanned Chicago Blackhawks club in six games. It took five games to eliminate the feisty Edmonton Oilers in round two. Forsberg led the way in the always-important first game of the Edmonton series, netting two goals and recording an assist in a 5–1 victory.

The Avalanche then found themselves facing off against their old nemesis, the Detroit Red Wings, in the Western Conference finals. The Wings had been waiting a year for a rematch. Behind the goaltending of Patrick Roy, the 'Lanche eked out a 2–1 victory in Game 1, even though the Red Wings outplayed them in every facet of the game. The Wings evened the series in Game 2, winning 4–2.

As the series shifted to Detroit, the Wings won a tight contest in Game 3, 2–1, and then blew out the Avalanche in Game 4, 6–0, to take a three-to-one lead in the emotional and bruising series. The

Avalanche returned the favor, winning 6–0 on home ice in Game 5, but the Wings took the series with a 3–1 victory in Game 6. What was sweet revenge for the Red Wings was bitter disappointment for Peter Forsberg and his Avalanche teammates, whose fine season ended sooner than they had anticipated.

Just as during the regular season, injuries hampered Forsberg during the playoffs. Coach Marc Crawford scratched him from the lineup in three games. His numbers were still respectable, however. In 14 playoff games, Forsberg scored 5 goals, 3 of which came on the power play, and had 12 assists. His plus/minus rating was a disappointing –6.

To recuperate from the difficult and grinding season, Forsberg relaxed in his spacious home in Golden, Colorado. He fished and played golf. He also returned again to Ornskoldsvik, where he maintained a summer home overlooking the Baltic Sea.

Forsberg certainly needed the rest, for during the next season, 1997–98, he played not only for the Avalanche, but also for the Swedish team in the 1998 winter Olympics in Nagano, Japan. For the first time, the NHL season paused so that many of the league's stars could compete in the Olympics for their home countries.

Peter's father, Kent, handled the coaching duties for the Swedish Olympic squad. As in the past, this arrangement did not seem to upset Peter in the least. In an interview he said that "at the rink, he's my coach. We don't talk about that he's my dad. He knows my moves. I'm glad he's on our team."

Although talented and determined, the Swedish team failed to repeat the heroics of the 1994 games.

The underdog Czech Republic took the gold in Nagano behind the superb goaltending of Dominik Hasek.

Returning to Colorado to finish the NHL season, Forsberg faced another disappointment when the Avalanche were quickly eliminated from the 1998 playoffs, losing to the Edmonton Oilers in the first round. Forsberg's own play, though, was brilliant. In that first round, he led all NHL players in scoring with 11 points, on 6 goals and 5 assists, in only 7 games.

Despite his recent injuries, setbacks, and disappointments, Peter Forsberg's play continues to mature and improve. Truly he has earned his nickname Peter the Great. He displays a winning combination of strong puck control, pinpoint passing, smooth skating, timely scoring, solid checking, and smothering defense. "There is nothing Forsberg can't do," wrote Sherry Ross in the *Hockey Scouting Report*, a book that profiles the strengths and weaknesses of more than 400 NHL players.

Forsberg is on the ice in all situations. He plays a regular shift, often centering Colorado's first line, flanked by left wing Valeri Kamensky and right wing Claude Lemieux. He also sees time on the power play; in the 1997–98 regular season, he scored 7 of his 25 goals with the man advantage. Furthermore, he kills penalties and plays four-on-four.

Occasionally, Forsberg has even demonstrated a little showmanship. In a game against the St. Louis Blues on March 11, 1998, for instance, he held on to the puck for an amazing 17 seconds as his team killed a penalty. As he zigged and zagged across the ice, St. Louis defenseman Chris Pronger slashed at Forsberg in frustration, earning time in the penalty box and thus negating the Blues'

Forsberg, playing for Team Sweden in the 1998 winter Olympics, tangles with Canadian player Chris Pronger. Although the Swedes played hard, they failed to repeat their Olympic triumph of 1994.

power play. The Avalanche went on to win the game, 3–2.

"When he's like that, he's fun to watch," said Blues coach Joel Quenneville. "Unfortunately, I had to watch." But Forsberg played down his show of finesse on the ice, even admitting that it had been "stupid" to hold the puck that long.

Recently, too, Forsberg has begun to emerge as a leader of the Avalanche on the ice and in the dressing room. "Peter has a great personality, a real dry sense of humor, and he can be a bit of a character," said his coach, Marc Crawford, "but he has never been particularly vocal, in the dressing room or on the bench." That hesitation to speak out began to disappear during the 1997–98 season, his fourth in the NHL. Forsberg has become more comfortable not only encouraging his teammates, but also criticizing their play when necessary and challenging them to do better. It is in the evolution of his leadership skills, Crawford thinks, that fans are "going to see the next level of improvement in his game."

Still, Forsberg is not without his critics. The general consensus is that he is too eager to pass and too hesitant to shoot. Many, such as teammate Claude Lemieux, believe that despite Forsberg's uncanny ability to pass the puck, his game has become too predictable. Opponents now anticipate that he will pass first and shoot only as a last resort. Players on other teams, observed Lemieux, "know that Peter is more of a passer than a shooter, and they cheat a little more on the pass." Forsberg "could score 50 goals if he wanted to," wrote Sherry Ross. He simply has to decide to shoot more often.

More serious criticism focuses on Forsberg's physical style of play. General Manager Glen Sather of the Edmonton Oilers described Forsberg as "great defensively, great

Face bloodied, Peter Forsberg watches as teammate Sylvain Lefebvre confronts a referee in the 1998 Stanley Cup playoffs. Despite Forsberg's strong play, the Avalanche were eliminated in the first round.

offensively, and hard to check," but went on to say that Forsberg is as "dirty as hell and . . . gets away with it because he's a big point producer." Others have also criticized his aggressive play and his seemingly arrogant attitude. Even his teammates and coaches must sometimes remind him to tone down his pugnacious defense when it interferes with his offensive game.

Peter has taken the criticism in stride. When asked about his aggressive streak, he simply replied, "I like it because you know you're in the game." Hockey "is a tough sport," he added recently. "You can't expect to go out there and not get hit." Marc Crawford agreed, stating that while there were many possibilities in Forsberg's future, "Peter will never win the Lady Byng," the award given annually to the player who exemplifies sportsmanship and good conduct on the ice.

Most close observers of the NHL do agree that Forsberg's rugged play has finally dispelled the notion that European players are soft. He dares opposing players to try to intimidate him, and his drive to succeed enables him to meet and overcome all challenges. "It's hard playing against him," conceded Edmonton Oilers defenseman Roman Hamrlik. "You have to take the body." Hamrlik's teammate, Drake Berehowsky, agreed, adding that Forsberg "definitely enjoys the physical stuff. He's a big boy who gives as much as he takes."

Just ask Boris Mironov, another Oilers defenseman, whose nose Forsberg broke with his stick in last year's playoffs. Or consider the case of Dallas Stars center Joe Nieuwendyk. In an early season game against Colorado, Stars defenseman Derian Hatcher bloodied Forsberg's mouth with a vicious elbow and was assessed a five-minute major penalty for roughing. Forsberg missed one

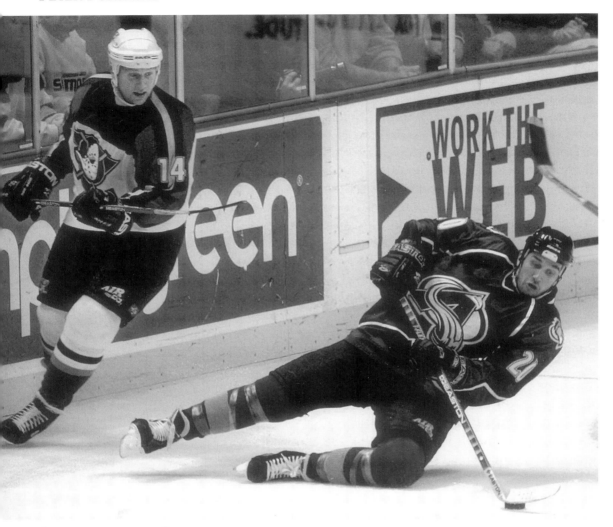

In a game against the Mighty Ducks of Anaheim, Forsberg hits the ice as he passes to a teammate. Some critics say he is too eager to pass rather than shoot.

shift (a player's turn on the ice) before returning to assist on a power-play goal. Later in the game, Forsberg leveled Joe Nieuwendyk with a clean and legal, but bone-jarring, check. Nieuwendyk missed 12 games with a bruised chest and a concussion.

Nevertheless, many coaches, including Ken Hitchcock of the Dallas Stars, have found that the

key to limiting Forsberg's effectiveness is to bad-
ger him until he loses his concentration and retal-
iates. "It's hard to stay composed, but I'm better
at it now that I was [in Sweden]," Forsberg admitted in a recent interview. Even his coach acknowl-
edged that it is a tough balancing act for Forsberg. "He's so competitive, he can get too riled up,
but we have to be careful not to take too much of
that away because that's the essence of his game."

Whatever criticisms may be leveled against him,
Peter Forsberg is widely regarded as one of the
NHL's most promising young stars. He is clearly
among the dominant figures in the game today,
and he shows no signs of letting up. The "Ultimate
Warrior," as one sportswriter dubbed him, stands
alongside the most talented and complete players
in the history of the National Hockey League.

All indications are that during the next few sea-
sons, four young players will dominate All-Star
games, trophy balloting, and perhaps the Stanley
Cup playoffs. They are Eric Lindros of the Philadelphia Flyers, Jaromir Jagr of the Pittsburgh Pen-
guins, and Paul Kariya of the Mighty Ducks of
Anaheim. The fourth member of that quartet will
undoubtedly be Peter Forsberg.

Statistics

Season	Team	Regular Season					Playoffs				
		GP	G	A	PTS	PIM	GP	G	A	PTS	PIM
1994–95	Que	47	15	35	50	16	6	2	4	6	4
1995–96	Col	82	30	86	116	47	22	10	11	21	18
1996–97	Col	65	28	58	86	73	14	5	12	17	10
1997–98	Col	72	25	66	91	94	7	6	5	11	12
Totals		266	98	245	343	230	49	23	32	55	44

GP   games played
G   goals scored
A   assists
PTS   points (goals plus assists)
PIM   penalties in minutes

CHRONOLOGY

1973   Peter Forsberg born on July 20 in Ornskoldsvik, Sweden.

1977   Begins skating at age 4.

1988   Makes television debut skating in *TV-pucken.*

1990   Begins skating for the MoDo team in the Swedish Elite League.

1991   Drafted by the Philadelphia Flyers as sixth pick of the NHL draft.

1992   Traded by the Flyers to the Quebec Nordiques as part of a package in exchange for Eric Lindros; Forsberg continues to play for MoDo.

1993   Plays in the World Junior championship for Sweden; wins Best Player award.

1994   Picked to play for Team Sweden in the 1994 Olympics in Lillehammer, Norway; in the gold-medal game against Team Canada, scores the game-winning goal in a shoot-out.

1995   Makes NHL debut with the Quebec Nordiques during the lockout season, scoring 50 points in just 47 games; wins the Calder Memorial Trophy for Rookie of the Year, 1994–95; named to the NHL All-Rookie Team.

1996   Playing for the relocated Nordiques, now the Colorado Avalanche, helps his team win the Stanley Cup; scores a hat trick in a single period against the Florida Panthers; selected for the NHL All-Star Game.

1997   Selected for the NHL All-Star Game, but replaced because of an injury.

1998   Named to Team Sweden for the 1998 winter Olympics in Nagano, Japan; again selected for the NHL All-Star Game.

FURTHER READING

Dater, Adrian. "Forsberg a Thrill Player." *The Hockey News*, March 27, 1998.

Dryden, Steve. "The Viking Warrior." *The Hockey News*, November 29, 1996.

Farber, Michael. "The Golden Goal." *Sports Illustrated*, March 7, 1994.

Farber, Michael. "Show Stoppers." *Sports Illustrated*, June 17, 1996.

Johnson, Paul M. "Hotshot: Peter Forsberg." *Sport*, February 1997.

McKenzie, Bob. "Fabulous Forsberg." *The Hockey News*, May 15, 1998.

Murphy, Austin. "Two Much." *Sports Illustrated*, December 9, 1996.

National Hockey League. *1996 NHL Yearbook*. Toronto: Worldsport Properties, 1996.

National Hockey League. *1997 NHL Yearbook*. Toronto: Worldsport Properties, 1997.

Olson, Gary. *Colorado Avalanche*. Mankato, Minn.: Creative Education, 1995.

Sullivan, Matt. "Colorado's Can-Do Kid." *Hockey Illustrated*, April 1997.

Wigge, Larry. "Gold Standard." *The Sporting News*, February 9, 1998.

Wigge, Larry. "Power Play." *The Sporting News*, March 25, 1996.

Wolff, Alexander. "Peter Forsberg." *Sports Illustrated*, February 7, 1994.

ABOUT THE AUTHOR

Meg Greene earned a bachelor's degree in history from Lindenwood College in St. Charles, Missouri, and master's degrees from the University of Nebraska at Omaha and the University of Vermont. She writes regularly for *Cobblestone Magazine* and other publications. Ms. Greene makes her home in Virginia.

INDEX